PROCRASTIMONSTERS!

They're everywhere

A story by **Claudia Hull**

PROCRASTIMONSTERS!
They're Everywhere

For information contact: Shalako Press
P.O. Box 371, Oakdale, CA 95361-0371
http://www.shalakopress.com

ISBN: 978-1-257-64007-2

Written by Claudia Hull
Illustrated by Toby Mikle
Cover format by Karen Borrelli

Dedicated to my own little
Procrastimonster!

(if he had not gotten in the way, this book would have been written sooner!)

This Book Belongs To:

"Josh! Josh, are you up yet?"
"JOSH! Get up now or you'll be late for school."
"I will. I will." Josh mumbled.

But he didn't. And he was late for school.

Josh was talking to his friends about a new movie
that was coming out. He didn't hear his teacher say,
"Last call for homework. Turn it in now or get
a zero in the grade book."

Josh kept talking to his friends.
And he got a zero in the grade book.

After school, Josh was supposed to mow Mrs.
Anderson's lawn.
She was going to pay him $10.00.
Josh looked at her lawn as he walked by,
it isn't that tall yet.
"It can wait." He thought.

So Josh didn't go over. And she hired someone else.

Josh walked into his kitchen, he noticed a note his
mom had left for him.
It said,

JOSH!

Please put dinner casserole

in the oven at 350 degrees.

It needs to cook for 1 hour.

Love, Mom

Josh thought, video game first.
There's plenty of time.
But he forgot, and there was no dinner.

Josh got ready for bed.
He went into the bathroom to brush his teeth.
But when he looked into the mirror, he screamed!
"Mom! Mom!" Josh yelled.
"There's something on my head!"

His mom came into the bathroom and said,
"There's nothing on your head.
Now quit stalling and get into bed."

"She can't see me." The thing on Josh's head said.

"What are you?" Josh asked.

"Me?" The thing teased.

"Why, I am the **Procrastimonster!**"

"The procrasti what?" Josh asked.

"The **Procrastimonster.**" The thing said again.

"And I am going to grow and grow.

I am going to stick with you forever.

Josh stared at the thing on his head.
"But I don't want you sitting on me."
"You're getting heavy!"

"But that's what I do. I'm here because you say
things like:"

In a minute.

I'll do it later!

Not right now.

"I love it when you say stuff like that. The more things you put off, the bigger I will get. I will be your best buddy!"

"No way!" cried Josh.
"Besides, I have to go to bed."

Josh tried to push the thing off his head.
He pushed, he pulled.
He even hung his head upside down.

The thing would not go away.
The Procrastimonster wouldn't budge.

"Awe, wouldn't you rather
go look through your telescope
or play on the computer?"

the Procrastimonster
whispered in his ear.

Josh looked at his telescope pointed out the window.
"I could look at the moon for a little while."
Josh thought.

And the **Procrastimonster** got a little bigger.

"Josh! Josh, are you in bed yet?"
his mom shouted up the stairs.

"In a minute mom!" Josh shouted back.
And the **Procrastimonster** got even bigger.

"Now cut that out!
Josh said to the thing on his head.

"No, this is fun!"
giggled the **Procrastimonster**.

Josh went to bed.
Maybe it will be gone in the morning.
But it wasn't. And it was very heavy.

"What are we going to put off doing today?" asked
the **Procrastimonster**.

Josh stared at the thing on his head.

"Nothing!" said Josh.

Josh went downstairs, ate some cereal and noticed
the chore list on the refrigerator.

"First, I'll get the weeds pulled." Thought Josh.

When Josh went outside…………

The **Procrastimonster** said,

"Hey, isn't that your soccer ball over there?"

"Come on, let's kick it around for awhile.

The garden can wait."

But Josh said, "No, it can't."
And Josh pulled all the weeds.

Josh needed to put his dirty clothes
in the laundry room.

The **Procrastimonster** said,
"Some of your friends are playing outside.
We could stay out for a little while longer?

"No, we can't" and Josh went inside and put his
dirty clothes in the laundry room.

And the **Procrastimonster**
got a little smaller.

The next morning,
Josh looked in the mirror.

The **Procrastimonster** was smaller.

And it didn't look very happy.

"Go away!" yelled Josh.

"No way." Said the Procrastimonster.

That weekend, Josh did all the things
he was supposed to do.

He got his backpack ready for school on Monday.

All his clothes were clean and put away.

Josh's mom asked him to set the table for dinner.

And Josh got right to it.

The Procrastimonster got even smaller.

After he said goodnight to his parents, Josh
washed his face and brushed his teeth.
When he looked in the mirror,
the Procrastimonster
was teeny, tiny.

"It's not supposed to be like this!"
whined the Procrastimonster.
"Oh yes it is!" said Josh. "Now, go away.
And go away NOW!"

The Procrastimonster shrugged its shoulders.
And disappeared.

THE END.

Can I be your best buddy?

Other Shalako Press Books
For Young Readers

Beam

Bonnie Bunny's Big Adventure

The Witch On Oak Street

Charlie Shepherd

Were You Born In That Chair?

Please visit us at www.shalakopress.com

CPSIA information can be obtained at www.ICGtesting.com
Printed in the USA
BVOW10s2348100215

387217BV00004B/12/P